The NEIGHBOURS

▶Factfile◀

Fascinating facts and inside stories – 'Neighbours' as you've never seen them before

NEIL WALLIS
AND
DAVE HOGAN

ANGUS
& ROBERTSON
PUBLISHERS

ANGUS & ROBERTSON PUBLISHERS

16 Golden Square, London W1R 4BN,
United Kingdom, and
Unit 4, Eden Park, 31 Waterloo Road,
North Ryde, NSW, Australia 2113

First published in the United Kingdom by
Angus & Robertson (UK) in 1989
First published in Australia by
Angus & Robertson Publishers in 1989

Text copyright © Neil Wallis 1989
Photographs copyright © Dave Hogan,
Syndication International and News Ltd 1989

Typeset in Great Britain by
New Faces, Bedford

Printed in Great Britain by
Scotprint Ltd, Musselburgh, Scotland

ISBN 0 207 16382 0

CONTENTS

1

WHERE DID THEY COME FROM?

This handsome lad can easily afford to pay someone to wash his car since he became a 'Neighbours' star. But who is he? Now he is laughing all the way to the bank over his good fortune, but things haven't always been so easy for this star.

He started life in a tiny seaside town called Shelley Beach, with a population of only 2000 and hundreds of miles away from the nearest city. He was jet-propelled into fame at the age of just sixteen. Long before 'Neighbours', a bored Sydney talent scout was visiting relatives in the New South Wales town and was dragged along to see the local High School's annual play. The leading role in the production of 'Oh What a Lovely War!' was played by a slim tall and goodlooking teenager who was very nervous. But afterwards the scout came back stage and told him, 'My son, I'm going to make you a star – as a top model.' A month later the country boy was installed as one of Australia's top TV and clothes models. But he hated it.

The lad, who is a natural laugh-a-minute joker missed his mum, his pet dog Scally, his surf-boarding mates, plus a green-eyed girl called Karen who was part of the same gang of schoolpals. So a year later, he recalls, 'I threw it all in and went home and became a plumber's mate.' And a brickie's mate, an electrician's mate, a roofer's mate ... he was even an apprentice bank clerk until he was fired after just nineteen days for completely wrecking the accounting system out of devilment. He even went back to washing cars for a while. Then came what turned out to be a lucky break. As a kid he was so tall and skinny his mates nicknamed him 'Dunny-brush' – Aussie slang for a loo brush. Hard to believe looking at this hunk today, but bullies used to torment him and kick sand in his face. Then Karen persuaded him to start weight-training so he could build himself up and start sticking up for himself. That good advice gave him the fantastic physique that send the girls wild to this day. It was also Karen who persuaded him to try acting again, with the local Shelley Beach Players. He was spotted yet again by another passing talent scout, and the rest is

'Neighbours' history. As a way of saying thank you, he married Karen and they lived together in the Dandenong Hills outside Melbourne. Sadly they recently drifted apart and separated. Who is he?

Answer: Craig McLachlan

Pushy could be this lady's middle name in her Ramsay Street role. And, as she is the first to admit, her strong will has got her into trouble for most of her real life too.

Hard to imagine to see her in the show, but she's the daughter of a very proper Melbourne bank manager, and she admits, 'My parents were horrified that I wanted to go on the stage – they wanted me to become a secretary and marry my boss.'

But that would never do for this lovely lady. While struggling to make a career in the theatre, she supported herself by modelling. ('That gave mum a few grey hairs, I was a real rebel.') She's always had an enormous sense of humour – despite what you might think from the show. She even kept smiling when her marriage (at twenty-six) to fellow actor David Ravenswood ended in divorce just three years later. In fact, they are still great friends.

Whatever you might think from the on-screen antics, everyone in 'Neighbours' loves this lady. She is particularly close to Kylie Minogue, who still calls her from all over the world to ask advice about her career.

And she is just as kind and concerned to non-Neighbours too. A year ago her cousin Suzanne died, leaving a twelve-year-old daughter, Emma orphaned. Typically, this 'Neighbours' star adopted her and took the teenager into her own home. Though that did cause problems of a different sort – this lady has a teenage son called Nicholas, who loves heavy metal music, Emma is a Bros fan. Our star is crazy about classical music – especially Vivaldi and Beethoven. So they all go in their different rooms with their own stereos and try and drown each other out!

A typical Capricorn, this is a lady who enjoys pampering herself. Every Saturday morning is set aside for giving herself a facial and having her hair done. She loves good food and fine wines – particularly French champagne. And if there's no particular man in her life to buy it for her she will buy it herself, that's the freedom that 'Neighbours' stardom has brought her. What is her name?

Answer: Anne Charleston

Strange to think that one of the biggest stars in 'Neighbours' was named after aboriginal slang for the boomerang. But that's what her name means!

This pretty little lady, born in Melbourne's

Bethlehem Hospital, was such a handful that her mother nicknamed her 'anklebiter' as a baby, but she is always guaranteed a warm welcome back wherever she appears, but particularly in Ramsay Street. And no one will be surprised that, despite all that fame, inside she's still the natural fresh kid she was when she first turned up at the 'Neighbours' studio in 1986.

She lives at home in the family house which her parents – her father is the chief accountant for the local council, her mother an ex-dancer turned housewife – bought in the 1970s. She has a sister (about whom, more later) and her brother is a TV technician.

That's where she still plays with her black pet pooch Gabby, and takes her turn feeding the tropical fish in the tank next to their special giant-screen TV with built-in video. She admits that her greatest pleasure apart from simply doing nothing and watching TV, is going shopping for clothes. (Her earliest memory is of a set of bootees her mum bought her for kindergarten. They were white vinyl with a zipper up the side and a black smiling face on the front – she thought them 'very trendy'.)

Her clothes are perhaps more appealing now – and in fact she's busy planning the launch of her own special designer range of clothes in time for Christmas 1989. Do you know who she is? (One more clue: she must be the only soap-opera superstar who, when she visited the legendary Harrods store in London for the first time, spent just £3.50 – on writing paper!)

Answer: Kylie Minogue

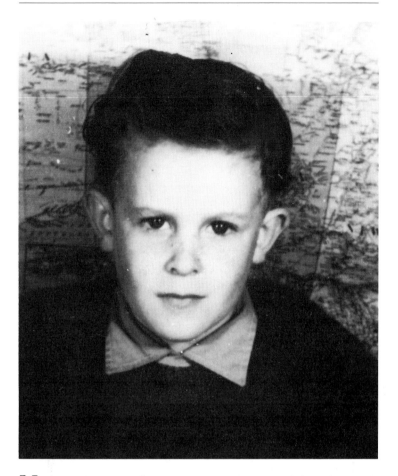

Hard to believe from the way he stumbles through life in 'Neighbours', but this clever boy always had a route to the top mapped out for himself. Always easy-going and ready to chat down Ramsay Street, this thoroughly nice guy does in real life suffer from crippling shyness.

In fact, that's why he became an actor in the first place – his mother made him take drama at Catholic Balmain High School, Sydney, to gain more confidence and soon he was winning most of the starring roles in the school plays, so it worked in one way at least!

Born with red hair and freckles, he comes from a working-class background. He remembers his father scrimping and scraping all year to buy him a trike at Christmas, and he was well into his teens before he was able to wear anything but hand-me-downs from his two elder brothers (he's also got an older sister). Never very academic, he hoped at first sport might become a career as he was a brilliant teenage rugby league prospect. But he was too good for his own good, and a dirty tackle from a desperate opponent shattered his collarbone and destroyed his sporting hopes forever.

This man is the thinker of the 'Neighbours' cast. He is very politically aware, and reveals that he is becoming increasingly religious. He collects antiques, and has started writing a novel which he hopes to get published this year. But not all his pleasures are highbrow – he loves setting up his full-size drumkit in his antiques-packed lounge and pounding away accompanying heavy-metal stars like Meatloaf and Led Zeppelin.

So who is this secret headbanger? (His pet loves are thunderstorms – and pussycats!)

Answer: Paul Keane

Few actresses can hold a candle to this 'Neighbours' star! Particularly when you realise just how different she is in real life from the sexy but very strait-laced character she plays down in Ramsay Street.

Her whole life has been topsy-turvy and contradictory. She lived the first eight years of her life in safe middle-class Melbourne, but was then taken to the back of beyond in the Australian outback when her parents divorced. In contrast to the surfing beaches and bright lights of the big city, she and her mother had to eke out an existence on a rough and ready smallholding in Chewton, near the famous mid-Victoria brewery town of Castlemain. There she became virtually vegetarian, eating home-baked bread, brown rice, and soya beans. While her former schoolfriends watched videos and went to the cinema, she had to clean out chickens and milk goats.

Her mother then remarried. Her new stepfather was an actor, and took her along to local drama groups – she can remember to this day the entire script of 'A Streetcar Named Desire' after

13

learning it at the age of fifteen when she was prompt for the local production. She was addicted to acting, and as soon as she was eighteen she ran away from home to go back to Melbourne to try and become an actress.

By day she was a waitress – often in some fairly sleazy dives – and by night she slaved away trying to make her acting name. But who is she? (P.S. At one stage, after teaching herself the tenor saxophone, she considered switching her career to becoming a jazz musician.)

Answer: Fiona Corke

This is one Little Bo Peep who has never lost any sleep over sheep. As a child she spent years living in sheep-farming country and absolutely hated it.

And even when she worried about her career before she landed a major role in 'Neighbours' she always used to console herself with the thought that at least acting was more fun than being trapped on one of those vast Australian sheep ranches.

She deserves her well-paid success in 'Neighbours', because she has truly had a very tough life. Her first husband was a bully who she had to throw out, then she had to struggle for seven years as a single mum to bring up their children, Tony and Jane. Then she remarried – and her second husband also occasionally appears in 'Neighbours'. (Her husband is much nastier on screen than off, because in real-life they're bigger lovebirds than Kylie Minogue and Jason Donovan could ever be, as she is the first to tell you.)

This well-spoken lady is a trained secretary who once worked in London for Kelloggs, the cornflakes people and spent years as a classical actress in the theatre. Now, during pauses between recording, she teaches the younger cast members in elocution. Her particular target is hunky Jason Donovan: 'He kept putting a "k" on the ends of his words, like "anythink". I soon put a stop to that.'

Who is she? (She's lovely and slim, but she still chuckles over the time she played the Fat Lady in a stage comedy. She wore a giant plastic hamburger round her waist, a hat made from liquorice allsorts and spaghetti and cakes on her chest, and doughnuts for earrings – she's never been able to fancy any of those things since.)

Answer: Anne Haddy

2
REAL-LIFE FAMILY AFFAIRS
OF THE NEIGHBOURS

This lovely young lady looks very familiar, but it's not 'Neighbours' and singing superstar Kylie Minogue with her hair dyed brown, in fact its her mum! And Kylie not only got her sensational looks from her mother Carol but also her talent and love for showbiz.

Born in Maesteg in South Wales and brought to Australia as a child when her family emigrated,

Carol was just sixteen when this picture was taken and already a talented dancer who won a host of cups and medals both as a ballerina and later as a Hot Gossip-style modern dancer. But she gave it all up at twenty to marry a serious-minded trainee accountant called Ron Minogue and bear him three children – Kylie first, then in 1970 brother Brendan and a year after that sister Danielle.

Kylie's childhood was gloriously happy. She first fell in love at junior school with a boy who helped her cheat in a spelling test to get the word 'bicycle' right! Even then she was a toddler, her school nickname was 'Shorty'. She remembers, 'I was too small for sport and rough 'n' tumble so Mum taught me how to sew and make things. While the other kids played tag I'd sit in my bedroom making way-out clothes or drawing. I was always getting told off at school for doodling on my homework books. I collected swapcards meticulously for years – I've still got them, I reckon they'll be worth a fortune one day.'

Despite her worldwide fame, and the millions that it has earned her, Kylie only ever feels totally at ease when she is back at home with her mum and family. She is also close to her Welsh granny. Wherever she is in the world, she talks by phone to her mother, and usually 'Grandma', every single day. And no matter how busy her schedule, the one vital date she always keeps with them all is 25 December.

Kylie explained, 'On Christmas Day *everyone* gets together in our family, it's an old Welsh tradition and it's sacred to us. And I would happily give up a Number One record rather than miss it.

'Mum's five brothers and sisters and their respective little ones, plus all the grandparents turn up. It's the greatest day of the year for me, and as I have got busier it's become ever more important. And most of all it means I can give my mum a lovely present, always something I have made her as well as something I've bought, and watch her expression as she opens it. It's my way of saying thank you to the lady who has made me what I am today.'

How do you avoid feeling left out when your beautiful and sexy sister is a famous TV star and pop singer, has her own line of ultra-trendy clothes named after her, and is making a fortune? Hard to believe now, perhaps, but that was the problem *Kylie* Minogue faced over her kid sister Danielle back in 1985!

At the time Dannii – as she is professionally known – was just fifteen but as the presenter of Australia's top pop and variety show 'Young Talent Time' was very big news. And despite her youth, she had the looks and figure that most models would kill for.

So it was very hard for Kylie, then seventeen but much plainer and more boyish looking, to cope with. Her early forays into children's TV in minor series like 'The Sullivans' and 'The Henderson Kids' seemed to have fizzled out. Then, after struggling to achieve her HSC, the Australian version of 'A' levels, she thought she'd have to resign herself to becoming a secretary. But, as one last try at showbiz she had longed to be in since she was three, she agreed to her agent's suggestion that she audition for a then-struggling soap opera called 'Neighbours' ...

Kylie says, 'I always wanted to match Dannii's success, but there was never any jealousy – just as there isn't now with *my* success. We've both just always wanted the other to do well. As kids we were more like twins than big sis and little sis anyway.' When Kylie got lonely during a promotional visit to Los Angeles last year, Dannii immediately flew out to her side. Together they went shopping down trendy Melrose Avenue and exclusive Rodeo Drive – and admit they spent thousands of pounds!

Both girls got infected with a love of pop music and performing at a very early age. Kylie recalls, 'We were always grabbing the hairbrush and pretending to be pop singers and dreaming a passing talent scout would hear us and make us big stars. Even then I used to write and sing my own songs.

We often played at being "ABBA" – I was always the blonde girl singer and made Dannii be the other one. Then mum took us all to see *Grease* and me and Dannii acted that out day after day for months.' In fact, the girls have sung together in public since – they performed 'Sisters' on Dannii's show during an anti-drugs concert. On the same show Kylie performed her first duet with Jason Donovan, singing the Howard Jones song 'No One Is To Blame'.

Jason Donovan had a very different family upbringing from the Minogue sisters. For his parents went through a very bitter divorce when he was just five. His British-born father, actor Terry Donovan brought him up virtually singlehanded until he married Jason's stepmother Marlene, and Jason spent years on film lots, in TV studios and backstage at theatres watching his father work.

Until Terry remarried, Jason had seen his real mother, Australian TV announcer Sue McIntosh, only for the occasional Christmas and birthday, but then that stopped altogether. He recalls, 'For some reason she cut me off completely, I never even got a birthday card. I never understood it, and didn't allow myself to care.' Until late last year, that is, when Jason decided to re-establish contact with her. She had remarried too and he had three half-sisters who were keen 'Neighbours' fans!

Jason has remained very close to his dad and feared it would be disloyal to see her, but though Terry has refused even to speak to Sue since their

Jason's mother – Sue McIntosh

divorce he was man enough to give his son his blessing.

Jason, who has a half-brother Paul from his father's second marriage, said, 'Yes, me and Mum are reunited now. I picked up the phone one day and just decided to ring her. It was wonderful and now we are close again.

'My three sisters are fabulous, I'm so glad to have them.' Katherine is thirteen, Olivia is ten, and baby Stephanie is just two – 'just old enough to coo

Young Jason and his dad spend Christmas together

and gurgle when she recognises me on the TV screen!' says Jason. And he found it hugely amusing when his mother told him she was once a glamour-girl 'Hills Angel' on the Benny Hill show.

Despite having no mum for so long, Jason grew up a self-confident young man. At fourteen he was heavily into punk and would sneak out at night to bluff his way into Melbourne's wilder nightclubs. He would leave home at dawn with his beloved 'Malibu' surf board to catch the waves down at his local beach – but would get so engrossed he would forget to go to school sometimes or arrive very late. But, after hardly studying at all for his last two years at school, he knuckled down and by working ten hours a day learnt the entire syllabus in just two weeks and passed his school exams with flying colours.

Not surprisingly, with his father being an actor, Jason did some child acting – notably in an Aussie mini-series called 'Skyways' – where he met a girl called Kylie Minogue ...

But his main ambition was to become a commercial artist and go into advertising. He knew, from his father's experiences, that acting is very precarious and wanted something solid to fall back on. Even now, though he earns an estimated $1,000,000 a year from 'Neighbours' and hit records, he is salting most of his cash away and still drives round in a twelve-year-old Volkswagen Golf!

3

WHO LIVES WHERE IN THE REAL-LIFE NEIGHBOURHOOD?

Charlene lives at Number 26 Ramsay Street in 'Neighbours'. But where does actress Kylie Minogue lay her head in real life? And where does her screen pal Mike Young (actor Guy Pearce) go home to at the end of a long hard day's filming? In the real-life neighbourhoods of the 'Neighbours' stars do they have a 'Waterhole' just round the corner to drop into for a quick schooner of Fosters? Or a Pacific Bank where they can find a friendly Des Clarke-style bank manager?

For that matter, are *they* good neighbours – as that distinctive theme song from the show urges? Just what are their own homes really like? Here are their real-life Ramsay Streets – all of them in Melbourne within an hour's driving distance of the famous Channel Ten studio where the show is recorded. In fact the stars are as universally liked off-screen as they are on, but, if anything, with even more interesting private lives than they portray for the TV cameras ...

Who lives behind the door of this $420,000 (£200,000) three-bedroomed bungalow in Turner Street, Armadale, a quiet small and secluded cul-de-sac? Openly placed next to a dustbin by the front gate is a box full of empty wine and champagne bottles. From inside loud rock music pounds out. And a large motorbike is on a stand by the front porch.

The answer, rather surprisingly, is Anne Charleston. And the roaring rock music and motorbike are there because she's got two teenage children.

As neighbour Damien Lynch, a twenty-seven-year-old TV cameraman said, 'The lady of the house is really very nice, very polite and friendly and even a bit refined – unlike the person she plays in the show.

'However, she does get harassed, just like Madge, but then anyone would with those two youngsters. Her nineteen-year-old is a typical "Neighbours" teenager actually. He plays his rock music very loud and at all hours, and whenever his mum's away he has all his mates round to play! He's what we call in Australia a "Petrolhead" because he is crazy about cars and doesn't care about anything else.

'He is always roaring up in some "new" secondhand car or other, then stripping it down in the middle of the street and rebuilding it or customising it and then selling it off. He is always leaving bits of rusty metal around. His mum yells at him, but unlike in the show he just ignores her – he's a bit of a handful.

'The girl is only fourteen but looks older. They are very close, and she's a lovely kid. But like any kid she likes pop, and she plays her stereo loud too. Then at the weekend mum has to compete against them both if she wants to hear her favourite classical music.'

But all the neighbours in Turner Street approve of the way Anne Charleston has recently improved the value of her white weatherboarded three-bedroomed home. She has put in a new bathroom suite, revamped her kitchen, and built an extension at the back. One thing she didn't change was the large lemon tree growing by the front door. She had it planted there to screen off the house from over-eager 'Neighbours' fans.

'She is a very considerate lady,' says Damien Lynch, 'if we ever want an autograph for a young relative she's always ready to oblige. And she knows it would inconvenience the rest of us if hordes of fans turned up so she likes to wear semi-disguises when she goes to or from the house.'

Down Ramsay Street, this very desirable hot property – his handsome looks and easy charm make him a worldwide pin-up – lives very modestly. But in real life, apart from Kylie Minogue's recent rocketing to riches via her pop records, he is probably far and away the wealthiest of the 'Neighbours' stars.

Accordingly Alan Dale lives in almost 'Dynasty' style in this very plush detached four-bedroomed residence with two matching brand-new cars in the driveways. Cowper Street, North Brighton is one of the most desirable areas of Melbourne. The house sits surrounded by beautiful trees in its own acre of ground in a lovely leafy wide road. It is worth more than $630,000 (£300,000), a huge amount of money by Australia's property price standards. Sharing it with him is one of the most glamorous women in Australia – model Tracy Pearson – and his two teenage sons.

And just as he is a popular figure down Ramsay Street, he is a big favourite in his own neighbourhood too. It is a Neighbourhood Watch area, and his neighbours keep an affectionate eye on his interests too. The elderly widow living next door explained, 'He is a simply lovely person who has been very good to me personally and to the rest of the street in general. My husband died recently and he couldn't have been kinder or more sympathetic. He made a point of coming round and offering to help in any way he could. So whenever I need anything doing round the house like moving heavy objects or changing lightbulbs I can't reach either he or his boys come round and do it for me. He never acts the big star or anything. He is a wonderful neighbour.

'And he is bringing up his sons so well. They never play their pop records too loud or tear up and down the street, and they are so nice and polite. He is a model father.'

It looks like a rundown church hall, but in fact this is the scruffy out-of-character home of one of 'Neighbours' biggest heart-throbs. The redbrick two-bedroom 'cottage' in Gibdon Street, Burnley, is the home of Jason Donovan. It's valued at about $273,000 (£130,000) because of its central Melbourne location. But even so it's hard to imagine why a major star would want to live here. There is a large

engineering factory on the opposite side of the busy dual carriageway, the front gate is hanging off and there are rubbish-filled dustbins in the front garden. But it's turned out to be a very good investment, for Jason bought it for just $164,000 (£78,000) two years ago, so he has really coined it and is now house-hunting for something bigger and better.

With him when he bought it was Jason's dad, the man whom Jason describes as 'my best friend in the world – I owe him everything'. And while this young householder runs around the world boosting his acting and singing career, it's been his father Terry who supervised the $42,000 (£20,000) of renovation work that has turned what was a rundown property into a perfect Yuppie pad. But often Jason and Terry get stuck in together knocking down walls and laying bricks and concrete. As next-door neighbour Mrs Helen Kallis says, 'He is a lovely boy and has worked very hard on his house whenever he is here. He is a sweet and considerate kid, he comes and apologises if he works late or makes a mess.

'Yes, I often see him there with his girlfriend, Kylie. She is so small and pretty. He told me she helped choose the wallpaper and the furniture. They go shopping or go to the launderette in the parade of shops at the end of the road together hand-in-hand. It's so sweet.'

In this young star's Ramsay Street home, there is barely room to swing a wombat. But in fact this superb mini mansion in Arundel Crescent, Surrey Hills is the home of Kylie Minogue. But though this young lady is raking in a fortune thanks to 'Neighbours' a lot of the credit for the smart

Minogue family lifestyle must go to her father, who is Chief Accountant with the local council (it's his signature on the hefty rates demands which drop through local letterboxes.) And he has managed his family's affairs so well that long before his daughter became a star they lived in this film star-style home.

Worth a good $840,000 (£400,000), it is a sprawling detached split-level four-bedroomed architect-designed home, cleverly built into a gentle hillside with large gardens front and rear. From the front it looks like a fairly ordinary modern bungalow, but from the very private tree-surrounded rear it is clearly a huge and lovely home. It looks out on a conservation area – a rolling wood with a pretty stream running through it. There is a specially built patio area that can only be seen from the air and that is where our star – and her equally pretty mother and sister – regularly sunbathe topless. Also living in the house is her brother Brendan, their pet dog Gabby, and a tank of tropical fish.

Neighbour Ross Hanney, a local businessman, says, 'The family are very popular down this street and always have been from long before "Neighbours". At one time, when the show first became a massive hit here in Australia, we'd get teenage fans rolling up in cars outside the house at all hours shouting for her, but she just ignored it and it eventually faded away.

'We don't see much of her, not least because this isn't the sort of area where people live in each other's pockets. We don't have street parties or that kind of thing and though there are three teenagers in that house there never seems to be any noise. For one thing the streets are very wide with lots of trees so usually you can only tell if someone is in by noticing a car in the drive!'

Another neighbour said, 'Sometimes she and her sister go out for walks in the woods chatting. But less so nowadays. We've had a couple of burglaries around here and she actually came home from a trip abroad one time to an empty house and disturbed an intruder. She was terrified, poor kid. It could have been very nasty. Luckily, he ran away.'

The owner of this house in Harrison Street, Box Hill is known to be one of the nicest people in the 'Neighbours' cast. He is Guy Pearce and he also owns one of the nicest homes of any of the young stars.

It's a relatively large two-bedroomed house with a sizeable garden, which – after all the renovations and work he has put into it since he bought it almost three years ago – is now worth about $285,000 (£135,000).

It is very much a young man's house, furnished with fashionable black wickerwork and laquered furniture. But his favourite room in the whole house is his second bedroom which he has converted into a musician's paradise. Because when he is not working on 'Neighbours', Guy just lives for playing and writing music – he was one of the founder members of the 'Neighbours' cast pop group.

Despite his being music mad, his constant playing and rehearsing never worry his neighbours down long and winding Harrison Street. It's a middle-class area, with a large Greek population who aren't afraid to make their own music when they want to. And the houses are set back in gardens and spaced well apart, with swathes of green grass verges bordering either side of the wide road.

So it's no surprise that neighbour Marisa Palmier, a twenty-six-year-old company representative says, 'He's music-mad and plays his guitar quite loudly at times but we are very tolerant around here. And even when his group is round rehearsing it doesn't go on too long or too loud.

'He has worked hard on the place and should be proud. For instance, he has built a new porch with his own hands.' She added with a hopeful giggle, 'He's a lovely guy – he will make some lucky girl a wonderful husband!'

Annie Jones, the owner of this house in Adderley Street, West Melbourne was in fact a real Plain Jane when she joined 'Neighbours' – but soon turns into a scheming glamourpuss marriage wrecker! But in real-life Annie couldn't be more different from the character she plays down Ramsay Street. She has lived openly for two years with her TV producer boyfriend in this two-bedroomed $335,000 (£160,000) cottage with its huge lounge and spacious well-fitted kitchen – she loves to cook special dishes like goulash for her boyfriend. The house might not look much, but this is very much one of Melbourne's growing Yuppie areas. And the fact that she lives on a busy main road opposite a large warehouse makes no difference.

For when that closes down at night the area comes alive with young people, students and the 'upwardly mobile'. Two minutes' walk away is a very nice little pub for the locals, just like The Watering Hole, and around the corner is a café just like the one Daphne used to run before her sad death. And lots of little one and two-man businesses are setting up in the area. But the area's increasing wealth isn't just attracting people like this 'Neighbours' star – it's also bringing in the crooks.

'We've been broken into twice, her once. Recently the phonebox across the road had the money stolen from its coinbox,' said her next-door neighbour Anna Bourozikas, a nineteen-year-old student.

'It's quite frightening to all of us – I've spoken to her about it a few times. She actually jokes that that doesn't happen down Ramsay Street, which shows what a good sport she is. Now she and her bloke have put security grills over all their windows to foil burglars and have bought a big ugly guard-dog. It goes crazy if anyone as much as leans on our fence never mind theirs, so hopefully it will work.'

Annie's house is many miles from the 'Neighbours' studio, so most mornings she is picked up by taxi at 6am and doesn't return until fourteen hours later. Then, if it is one of Melbourne's fine light evenings, she and her boyfriend will un-padlock their cycles and ride round to one of the many local bistros or winebars for dinner with friends. Far more sophisticated than anything she ever gets up to in 'Neighbours'!

It is hard to believe that the 'Neighbours' character played by the star who owns this house would ever have the gumption to get himself married – but in fact Harold Bishop does just that.

In real life Ian Smith has been a doting husband for years. It is his great sadness that he is not a father too. And in fact he and wife Gail bought this lovely three-bedroomed home with just that in mind. But heartbreaking medical problems meant it was never to be.

Now they live as a tender twosome in this sprawling $370,000 (£175,000) bungalow in Buxton Street, Elsternwick, and devote their time to each other and to the local community. For Ian, more than any of the other stars, takes a very active part in neighbourhood life.

If his TV schedule allows, he will take part in local road safety campaigns, was a leading light in a move to form a local anti-crime Neighbourhood Watch scheme, and takes a deep interest in what his neighbours are up to. Quite apart from caring for his often-ailing wife.

One of Ian's neighbours, Voula Karatzas, an eighteen-year-old student, said, 'They're unable to have children, which is very sad as he'd make a great dad. He has always been available to us for help or advice, for instance. He asks my parents when my exams are, and then makes a point of asking me if I am studying enough and so on. Then he remembers to ask how I did and is genuinely interested in the answer.

'He loves gardening, and we often natter over the fence. He is a big fan of barbeques, sometimes for just him and Gail, other times for his TV friends or even just us neighbours. He has always made time, not just for me but for all the local kids as well. He always takes time to give autographs, and if we have relatives visiting who want to meet a "Neighbours" star he never minds at all.

'He does everything he can for Gail, because she is in poor health. I used to work part-time as a checkout girl in the local supermarket. Often he will come home from a long day at the studio then go out to do the shopping even though she doesn't work. He does quite a lot of the cooking too, I believe, and never minds giving a helping hand with the housework.' Which all sounds very like Harold Bishop!

40 THINGS YOU NEVER KNEW ABOUT THE NEIGHBOURS STARS

Can you list Kylie Minogue's pet hates? What was 'The Mousepack' and which 'Neighbours' star was in it? Who in the show does Anne Charleston reckon is 'a right cow?' Which Ramsay Street regular used to spend their summer holidays at Skegness in Lincolnshire? How much does it cost to make a single episode of the show?

Here are the answers to these and many more intriguing questions.

☆ Both the Queen and Princess Diana are known to be 'Neighbours' fans – but did you know that Princess Diana confessed to a Londoner last year that Prince William was also hooked?

☆ 'Neighbours' was first screened at 6pm on 18 March 1985 on Australia's Channel Seven. It was dropped after 171 episodes, revamped and brought back on Channel Ten all in that same year. It was first broadcast in Britain on 26 October 1986.

☆ The show was shifted from its initial midday placing to twice daily primetime slots on 1 January

1988 by the then BBC1 Controller Michael Grade after his sixteen-year-old daughter Alison told him how she and her pals risked daily detention by sneaking into their school's computer room to watch the show.

☆ Why is the show so successful? A Sydney University Sociology Professor's view is: 'It has the genuine sense of community spirit which we all crave, and a tempo and rhythm which matches out own lives.' On the other hand **Elaine Smith** (who played Daphne) reckons the five-nights-a-week show succeeds because 'it has a little comedy, a little drama, a little love, a little everything'.

☆ So just what are **Kylie's** pet hates? Brussels sprouts, snails and 'any other creeply-crawly', flying, and rudeness.

☆ **Stefan Dennis** had a very strange home life as a boy. His mum divorced his sea captain father and remarried, but then she and her new husband allowed Stefan's dad to come and live with them for months at a time whenever he was home from sea!

☆ **Lisa Armytage** caught fleas when she spent her honeymoon on a houseboat in Kashmir.

☆ **Vivean Gray** says of her meddling character Mrs Mangel: 'If I met *her* in real life I'd probably be very rude to her – she's horrible!'

☆ **Peter O'Brien** was so broke that he was reduced to teaching rich kids to surf when he heard he had passed his 'Neighbours' audition. Even so, he finished his day's instruction before going off to celebrate.

☆ **Jason Donovan** might look hopeless around the house as Scott in 'Neighbours', but in fact he cooks a mean omelette and can even do a full Sunday roast. And he has known how to do his own washing since he was eight.

☆ **Alan Dale** is hooked on vintage sports cars. In recent years he has owned, among other things, an MGB GT, a Mercedes two-seater, six different Jaguars, a Morgan and a Mazda RX. Perhaps he got his taste for fast vehicles from his days in New Zealand as a milkman driving an electric milkfloat!

☆ **Kylie** dreams of owning a huge 1950s open-topped American Thunderbird car, but has to settle for a wheezing four-door Honda hatchback. She daren't risk attracting the attention that her dream motor would be bound to draw.

☆ **Guy Pearce** was once threatened with a knife by the jealous boyfriend of a besotted girl fan who had stopped and asked him for his autograph!

☆ Each 'Neighbours' show costs just $55,000 (£25,000) to make, half the cost incidentally of 'Eastenders'. The scriptwriters get just $1700 per episode – and Ian Smith who plays Harold, has it written in his $2,000-a-week contract that he writes at least one script a month.

☆ **Elaine Smith** was born in Largs, Scotland, but only lived there for eighteen months before her family emigrated to South Africa. They moved on to Australia in 1975.

☆ **Ally Fowler,** who used to play Jim Robinson's girlfriend Zoe Davis, has become an Australian pop star with her group 'The Chantoozies' after quitting 'Neighbours'.

☆ **Kylie's** smash-hit single 'I Should Be So Lucky' sold an astonishing 1.7m copies (600,000 in Britain) worldwide.

☆ Do you remember that the first Lucy Robinson's real christian name was Kylie?

☆ **Vivean Gray** spent the first twenty-three years of her life in England, and was born and brought up in

Lincolnshire. So not surprisingly it was she who used to spend all those summer hols on the bracing beaches of Skegness!

☆ **Craig McLachlan** used to teach body-building and physical fitness to women, and even used to take their aerobic classes. He admits that 'sometimes it was very difficult to keep my mind on the job – particularly when they came and asked me to give their deltoids the once over! What can a man do?'

☆ **Ian Smith** had a collection of seventy pipes, including one worth $700 (£300), but threw them all away when his doctor warned him to give up smoking. Now he is collecting hats.

☆ **Stefan Dennis** once escaped a mugging because the gang of six teenage robbers recognised him and settled for autographs instead.

☆ **Kylie's** favourite subjects at school were art, technical drawing, sociology and needlework. But she hated maths – which is a pity, considering all the money she has to count these days.

☆ The 'Neighbours' theme song is sung by Barry Crocker, but was composed by Tony Hatch – the man who produced the music for the former British soap opera 'Crossroads'. It earns him £350 a week from the show, plus tens of thousands of pounds more from the various records which have been made of it. He now lives in Australia.

☆ **Annie Jones's** favourite actress is Jessica Lange: Fiona Corke admires Audrey Hepburn; Lisa Armytage adores Meryl Streep.

☆ The criminal past of his character Henry nearly landed **Craig McLachlan** in a bar-room brawl with a drunken ex-jailbird. Craig recalls, 'He was a gorilla with tattoos on his tattoos. He was yelling he had been in more prisons than "Henry" and was tougher and he'd prove it! When he marched over with his gang I thought we were dead meat.' However Craig, as quickwitted in real life as Henry is in Ramsay Street, cracked a few jokes at his own expense and bought a few drinks and the aggro ended.

☆ The 'cow' whom **Anne Charleston** was talking about in 'Neighbours' is her character Madge!

☆ **Kylie** got hooked on bangers and mash during her first trip to Britain when she visited some relatives of her mother in Wales.

☆ Music-mad **Guy Pearce** can play piano, saxophone, clarinet, guitar and synthesiser. And he can sing as well. His favourite pop star is Kate Bush – his music room is covered with posters of her.

☆ Poor **Anne Haddy** is finding it hard at the moment to work out what is fact and what is fiction. In an episode not yet seen in Britain she suffers a terrible stroke and is only saved by the quick thinking of Doctor Beverly. Her screen family fears she might have to have a major life-risking operation. Whereas in real life she has twice had to undergo open-heart surgery and also had major surgery on her stomach as a result of a cancer threat. Incidentally, for health reasons she has not eaten red meat since 1979.

☆ **Jason Donovan's** favourite holiday spot is Hawaii – but the price of his worldwide fame is that he hasn't been able to have a proper vacation for two years.

☆ **Craig McLachlan** went to a Michael Jackson concert as an ordinary fan, and ended up getting mobbed. He had to run to Security for safety; they smuggled him out of the stadium and he never did get to see the concert.

☆ **Guy Pearce** cast off his boy-next-door image in his Australian Big Screen debut 'Heaven Tonight'. He plays Paul Dystart, the successful, raunchy pop singer son of failed former rock star Johnny Dystart. Guy sings the single 'Jeopardy' on the soundtrack that was released to coincide with the film.

☆ Thank Batman for 'Neighbours'! For an adventurer called John Batman founded the settlement that was to become Melbourne in 1835.

☆ **Paul Keane** used to work as a storeman, **Alan Dale** was a disc jockey, **Anne Charleston** has been a model, **Anne Haddy** was once employed as a shorthand typist, and **Vivean Gray** spent several years as assistant matron in a boys' public school.

✧ **Danielle Minogue** isn't sitting back and leaving all the success to her big sister – she is playing the headstrong daughter of an Australian MP in a lavish series called 'All The Way'. Their brother Brendan also loves show business but is much more shy and works as a TV cameraman.

☼ 'Neighbours' is about to get a new star! He is **Ashley Paske,** who has been seen in Britain before in 'Richmond Hill'. He plays eighteen-year-old Matt Robinson, a cousin that Scott never knew he had. He soon starts to cause problems for Craig McLachlan's character Henry by developing a crush on his girlfriend Bronwyn.

☼ What was 'The Mousepack'? It was what **Peter O'Brien** mockingly dubbed himself and his acting pals after a pretentious but well-meaning showbiz writer described them as Australia's version of the famous Hollywood Ratpack. As Peter says, 'It's important not to start believing the publicity in this game.'

☼ Who is sensible Dr Beverly's favourite composer? Mozart, Chopin possibly? Or even Val Doonican? No, actually it is American rock idol Bruce Springsteen! She has got every single and album he has ever made.

☼ Do you know exactly *why* 'Neighbours' is so funny? Because it is part of the deal that Channel Ten agreed with the Grundy Organisation when it bought the show over from Channel Seven that 'humour' be a component of the script. Which is why when Clive Gibbons quit the show, he was replaced by genuinely zany Craig McLachlan.

5

THE NEIGHBOURS OFF-DUTY

FIONA CORKE

Although very much a girl of today, she is mad about the 1950s and early 1960s and has a huge collection of original Teddy Boy era records by Buddy Holly, Eddie Cochrane and many others. Give her a chance, and she'll show you how she can jive! She's also a collector of expensive Art Deco lamps, which adorn her two-storey Melbourne apartment.

Another passion is Mexico, where she stayed for three months during a round-the-world backpacking trip before returning to Australia. Ever since, she's been hooked on spicy Mexican food like tortillas and enchiladas and has even taught herself to cook them. She boasts her chili is the meanest in all Australia – and always serves it with jugs of iced water! One man who has tried it and lived to tell the tale is boyfriend Nick Carrafa, a fellow actor who has recently appeared in 'Neighbours' as hunky motor mechanic Tony Romeo.

Another hangover from that trip is that Fiona is crazy over Latin American music and jazz. She has even taught herself to play the saxophone and has jam sessions sometimes with other young members of the 'Neighbours' cast. She is a self-confessed whacky lady who loves scouring junk shops for all kinds of strange items. She has two lifesize shop dummies in her lounge, one of which wears bra and girdle, the other a joker's outfit! Plastic oranges and bananas hang from her pot plants, and bizarre puppets dangle from chairs and tables. She has a pet parakeet, which she allows to fly freely around the house. Her taste in clothes match her apartment. She is famed on the 'Neighbours' set for her wayout earrings, leopard-pattern peddlepusher pants and sombrero hats.

GUY PEARCE

On-screen, he is a jazz musician. Off-screen, he wants to be a real-life rock star.

In his private life Guy Pearce devotes all his spare time, and most of his money, to achieving that ambition. English-born Guy is actually considering quitting 'Neighbours' to launch himself into a music career in London. And he gets so much pleasure out of music that he doesn't care if he fails. He explains, 'You come home after a long wrenching day at the set and it's relaxing to sit for hours at the piano and tinker with different ideas. I write songs, do arrangements. My best mate from the show Craig McLachlan, who is also mad on music, comes over and we jam together.'

Guy is luckier in love off-screen than he is on. He has been going out with childcare nurse Shaney Stone for almost three years. They live a quiet life, not least because she finds the attentions of all the

Right: *The sky's the limit! Kylie works out for one of her more famous dance routines.* Below: *Kylie gets the make-up treatment*

The 'Neighbours' cast pose together before their performance at the Royal Variety Show – Christmas 1988

Australia and Britain's number one pin-up – Jason Donovan

Jason is not going to be Scott Robinson for the rest of his life –
he's the star of 'Heroes' as well as 'Neighbours'

Sometimes even superstars like Kylie Minogue have to look after their own luggage …

Craig McLachlan, ex-plumber's mate, ex-bank clerk, now much better known as Henry Ramsay

Peter O'Brien – Shane has turned into a suave star of stage and screen

Three heads are better than one! Henry, Jane and Paul, played by internationally recognised heart-throbs Craig McLachlan, Annie Jones and Stefan Dennis

girl fans who are drawn to lean and handsome Guy to be a problem. Much of the time they spend at his home, where, when he is not playing music, he is usually listening to something romantic by Kate Bush or Peter Gabriel. Guy also loves body-building – when he was sixteen he won the title Teenage Body-Building Champion of his home state of Victoria. He says, 'I've let myself go a bit because "Neighbours" and my music is so demanding, but whenever I can I pump iron three hours a day, six days a week. I love it, once I start I can't stop. I hope one day to have a gym in my house.'

CRAIG McLACHLAN

Surfing, weight-training, housebuilding, playing guitar ... how does he pack it all in on top of working *sixty* hours a week in 'Neighbours'? Plus the regular and lucrative personal appearances that an in-demand star like this man gets asked to make several times a week? His typically jokey answer is 'very little sleep'. Plus, until recently, the support of his lovely wife Karen. When she moved from their old home in Sydney to join him in Melbourne after he became established as a major 'Neighbours' star they bought a big old house outside Melbourne which they were lovingly renovating. Craig has remained there since the marriage break and his new romance with Rachel Friend. Pride of place goes to a special music room so he can continue the love of rock music that began when he was thirteen playing lead guitar for a High School group. At fifteen he was taking off to the nearest big town and sneaking into clubs to play rock, even jazz-funk with older guys. He even played in a punk band for a few weeks but was booted out for refusing to have a safety-pin through his nose or his nipples pierced!

Then he formed his group Alex Clegg and the Y-Fronts. Craig recalled, 'We used to wear Y-Fronts *over* our jeans, we thought it was really hip. Somehow we never really got very far, though we had loads of fun – which is really what life is all about, isn't it?'

He still plays several nights a week, usually with his closest pal from the cast, Guy Pearce. They were together in the 'Neighbours' pop band and are working together seriously on writing songs and putting together a real band with which they hope to make records and tour.

When Craig isn't playing or listening to music, he loves to continue the surfing which he first learnt in the seaside town where he was brought up. He also puts in a couple of sessions a week weight-training – which is how he keeps that fantastic body in trim. The work he has to do in clearing the acre of ground surrounding his house, which had been allowed to become totally overgrown, is also very physically demanding.

Another Craig hobby is practical jokes. Like the time when he lived near a golf course and whenever a ball landed in his garden he'd break a fake blood capsule and claim he'd been injured! Or the time he turned up on the 'Neighbours' set to play a love scene with his on-off girlfriend Bronwyn and went to kiss her wearing Dracula fangs!

STEFAN DENNIS

This handsome man has really cooked up a storm in 'Neighbours' – and he loves to do just the same at home. For Stefan Dennis trained as a chef and, despite finding acting stardom, it has remained his hobby. Stefan, unlike the hard-headed Paul Robinson in the show, is another Neighbours Nutter. Once he walked out on a job as a chef after just two days because the staff weren't zany enough, and another time ate a cigarette on a charity anti-smoking TV programme!

He met his wife Roz Roy, a leggy brown-haired model, when they both worked in a gay bar in Melbourne. He recalls, 'Once the customers realised we were in love they stopped chatting me up and started sending her chocolates.'

They live in a magnificent 1920s house in two acres of ground in the Dandenong Hills outside Melbourne. It is surrounded by thick trees to keep away amorous fans. There they spend almost all of Stefan's off-duty time swimming in their heated outdoor pool or playing with their Alsatian dog Sook, their Siamese cat and two goats.

Stefan, one of the few surviving actors from the original 'Neighbours' show before it was relaunched with Kylie Minogue and others to become the worldwide hit it is today, admits that the programme has made him a wealthy man. And he likes nothing better than to spend his hard-earned cash on sports cars – like a Saab Turbo – and living the high life with wife Roz.

ANNIE JONES

She is a beautiful former cover girl who looks as though she is made of porcelain. But in fact few people on the show are as tough as this lady, both mentally and physically.

For instance, her idea of a fun day out is to wade thigh deep into a raging river and stand there fishing for hours! Not something, somehow, you can see her character Jane Harris doing ... But Annie explained, 'My father is a great fisherman and used to take me along and I got the bug. I adore the peace and the quiet, and the satisfaction it gives you. It's mental exercise too, you have to think the fish onto your hook. Once I even went angling in the Crocodile Dundee territory. Now that was fun, but very scary as well I must admit.'

And after a day's fishing? A huge Italian meal with her live-in boyfriend, 'I know it's fattening but it's an absolute passion with me. Garlic bread, spaghetti, lasagne, lovely Italian wine ... wonderful. Then home to listen to some David Bowie or Ricky Lee Jones. That's the way to this girl's heart.' Otherwise she and her boyfriend spend their time walking their red-haired Kelpie guard-dog Roy, driving their open-topped Landrover over as tough terrain as possible, or going for long bike rides.

6

THE NEIGHBOURS FAMILY TREE

No matter how long you watch 'Neighbours', it becomes very hard to remember exactly who is related to who and how. What precisely is Max Ramsay's relationship to Scott? Who was Paul Robinson's first wife? Can you name the half-sister of Des Clarke? The answers are all below in the 'Neighbours' Family Tree.

The Ramsays

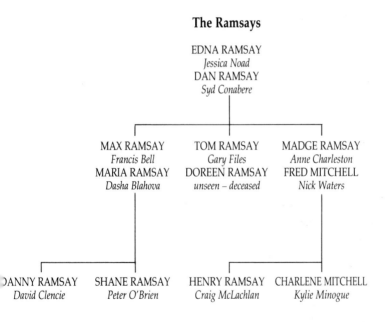

EDNA RAMSAY
Jessica Noad
DAN RAMSAY
Syd Conabere

MAX RAMSAY
Francis Bell
MARIA RAMSAY
Dasha Blahova

TOM RAMSAY
Gary Files
DOREEN RAMSAY
unseen – deceased

MADGE RAMSAY
Anne Charleston
FRED MITCHELL
Nick Waters

DANNY RAMSAY
David Clencie

SHANE RAMSAY
Peter O'Brien

HENRY RAMSAY
Craig McLachlan

CHARLENE MITCHELL
Kylie Minogue

The Robinsons

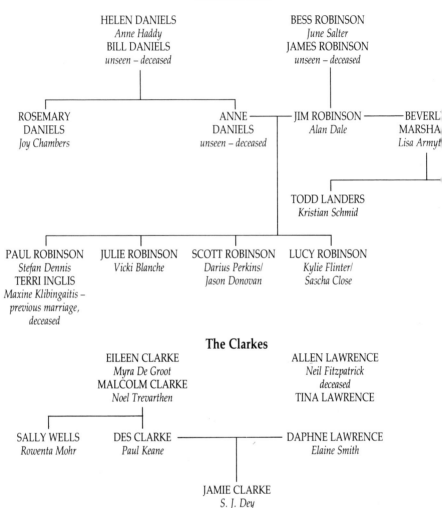

HELEN DANIELS
Anne Haddy
BILL DANIELS
unseen – deceased

BESS ROBINSON
June Salter
JAMES ROBINSON
unseen – deceased

ROSEMARY
DANIELS
Joy Chambers

ANNE
DANIELS
unseen – deceased

JIM ROBINSON
Alan Dale

BEVERL
MARSHA
Lisa Armyt

TODD LANDERS
Kristian Schmid

PAUL ROBINSON
Stefan Dennis
TERRI INGLIS
*Maxine Klibingaitis –
previous marriage,
deceased*

JULIE ROBINSON
Vicki Blanche

SCOTT ROBINSON
*Darius Perkins/
Jason Donovan*

LUCY ROBINSON
*Kylie Flinter/
Sascha Close*

The Clarkes

EILEEN CLARKE
Myra De Groot
MALCOLM CLARKE
Noel Trevarthen

ALLEN LAWRENCE
*Neil Fitzpatrick
deceased*
TINA LAWRENCE

SALLY WELLS
Rowenta Mohr

DES CLARKE
Paul Keane

DAPHNE LAWRENCE
Elaine Smith

JAMIE CLARKE
S. J. Dey

The Dennisons
LAURA DENNISON
Carol Skinner
TOM DENNISON
unseen – deceased

NIKKI DENNISON
Charlene Fenn

The Youngs
BARBARA YOUNG
DIANA GREENTREE
DAVID YOUNG
Stewart Faichney

MIKE YOUNG
Guy Pearce

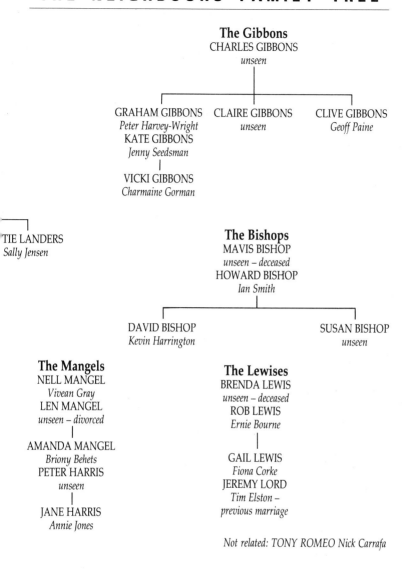

The Gibbons
CHARLES GIBBONS
unseen

GRAHAM GIBBONS
Peter Harvey-Wright
KATE GIBBONS
Jenny Seedsman

VICKI GIBBONS
Charmaine Gorman

CLAIRE GIBBONS
unseen

CLIVE GIBBONS
Geoff Paine

TIE LANDERS
Sally Jensen

The Bishops
MAVIS BISHOP
unseen – deceased
HOWARD BISHOP
Ian Smith

DAVID BISHOP
Kevin Harrington

SUSAN BISHOP
unseen

The Mangels
NELL MANGEL
Vivean Gray
LEN MANGEL
unseen – divorced

AMANDA MANGEL
Briony Behets
PETER HARRIS
unseen

JANE HARRIS
Annie Jones

The Lewises
BRENDA LEWIS
unseen – deceased
ROB LEWIS
Ernie Bourne

GAIL LEWIS
Fiona Corke
JEREMY LORD
*Tim Elston –
previous marriage*

Not related: TONY ROMEO Nick Carrafa

THE RAMSAYS

MAX Almost the father figure of 'Neighbours' in the early days, he is the head of the Ramsay clan and Madge Mitchell's brother. He is terribly proud of the fact that Ramsay Street is named after his grandfather. Essentially a nice guy, but he can be somewhat domineering at times and often seems hard-headed and unmoving. He became so totally wrapped up in his one-man plumbing business it cost him his marriage when neglected wife Maria (played by Dasha Blahova) walked out and ran away to Hong Kong. She did return home for a while but it was never the same.

Max is played by Francis Bell, who has starred in famous films like *Breaker Morant* (with stars like Edward Woodward, now of 'The Equaliser') and many Australian mini-series and TV serials. His hard-man looks mean he is a favourite for TV detectives.

SHANE Max's son, his father's obsession with him becoming a champion diver meant he had a tough childhood. It left him with an independent spirit, but fortunately he remained easygoing and a genuine nice guy. More the strong silent type than a silver-tongued Don Juan, he still somehow seemed to break the hearts of most of the available women who strolled down Ramsay Street. Somehow Shane was always in trouble, usually because of his beloved motorbike.

In real life Peter O'Brien, the actor who played Shane, is also a motorbike nut. Before 'Neighbours', he starred in several Australian films and TV serials. He is a qualified teacher and used to be seen riding his motorbike to and from work. Peter quit 'Neighbours' a year ago and now stars in the hit BBC TV series 'Flying Doctors'.

MADGE Max's older sister is a fiery-tempered no-messing lady who went back to using her maiden name to escape being linked with debts run up by her scoundrel ex-husband Fred Mitchell (played by Nick Waters). They have a son and daughter who both cause her endless trouble and heartache. She works as a barmaid at the Lassiters hotel complex. Still very attractive, she once tried to start a relationship with Jim Robinson but he was too young for her. Then childhood sweetheart Harold Bishop came back to Erinsborough and they soon became an item once more. Madge is played by veteran screen actress and former top model Anne Charleston.

HENRY Madge and Fred's eldest child, and Ramsay Street's resident prankster. He arrived back at Ramsay Street after serving a jail sentence for taking part in a robbery, and though he has served his time he lives under a constant cloud of suspicion from some of his unforgiving neighbours. Henry is very streetwise and always on the lookout for easy money, though he makes sure he – just! – stays on the right side of the law. He is constantly coming up with some new bright idea or daft scheme to make a fortune, and though they never seem to come off he is irresistible. He likes to fancy himself as a ladies man, and has good cause! Played by Craig McLachlan.

CHARLENE She lived with her dad Fred in Coffs Harbour, New South Wales, after her parents' divorce. She only came under protest to live with

Madge in Erinsborough when her father found he was incapable of looking after her. Famous for her quick temper whenever she thought someone was trying to pull a fast one at her expense. Her life was one long series of scrapes and scraps with her equally strong-willed mum. But really she is a thoroughly nice kid with a heart of gold, the sort who automatically sides with the underdog. Charlene tried to settle down after her marriage to Scott Robinson, working hard to complete her apprenticeship as a motor-mechanic. But it couldn't last ... The role of Charlene opened the door to worldwide stardom for young actress Kylie Minogue. Before she landed the part she had been a moderately successful child actress, but hadn't worked for a while and was considering abandoning her dreams of showbiz and becoming a secretary. She quit 'Neighbours' in mid-1988 to concentrate on her rocketing pop career, but the door has been left open for her to return if she ever wants to.

THE ROBINSONS

JIM One of the most popular characters in 'Neighbours', he is a caring and understanding dad who, after his wife Anne died (after giving birth to their fourth child, Lucy) devoted his life to looking after his children. He is a qualified engineer who is a partner  in a small but successful engineering firm. He finds it hard to express his feelings, but after the years of loneliness he may have found happiness at last in the arms of lovely Dr Beverly Marshall. The part is played by New Zealander Alan Dale, who started in show-business as a top disc-jockey in Auckland and Australia before moving into acting in various films and TV serials. Sports mad, Alan enjoys boxing, cricket, water-polo, water skiing and sailing.

PAUL He started out as the quiet member of the family, but he became bitter and self-centred after his first wife Terri Inglis (played by Maxine Klibingaitis) first tried to defraud him and then attempted to have him murdered! She was jailed as a result. Once an air steward, he has become a successful businessman and is now running the Lassiters complex as the hard-nosed head of the Australian end of the Daniels Corporation. But his ruthless approach has shocked his family and won him the nickname 'JR' after the antics of that infamous TV 'Dallas' oilman. He has recently found happiness on a personal level by remarrying, but his continued bitterness over his marital experiences first time round mean the new relationship has its stormy moments. Paul is played by Stefan Dennis, a regular from a whole string of well-known Australian television shows.

SCOTT The male pin-up of 'Neighbours', he broke every female heart in Ramsay Street when he finally married on/off/on/off girlfriend Charlene Mitchell last year. He was still at school when he got married but at first he seemed to accept his new responsibilities well. But then he began to go off the rails a little, going boozing with brother-in-law Henry. Then other temptations arose. He is very close to his dad

Jim Robinson, but relationships are more strained with big brother Paul. Since leaving school he has begun a career as a trainee journalist. The part was played originally by Darius Perkins, but after a series of rows with the producers he was dropped from the programme in late 1985. His replacement was Jason Donovan, son of well known actor Terence Donovan. Jason has starred in 'Skyways', 'I Can Jump Puddles', 'Home', 'Marshlands' and 'Golden Pennies'.

LUCY The apple of Jim Robinson's eye, she is a happy even-tempered tomboy. Her mother died very soon after she was born so Lucy has looked to her grandmother, Helen Daniels, as a mother figure. She has reached an age now where interests in boys and clothes begin to show. To daddy's evident distress, she is growing up and, after a trip to Paris, is blossoming into a young woman. Originally played by child actress Kylie Flinker, but later the role was taken over by Sascha Close, a trained ballerina and former drama school student.

HELEN DANIELS Jim's mother-in-law has been a tower of strength since the death of her daughter Anne. Nicknamed the 'Rock of Gibraltar' in the Robinson household, she is always ready to dispense kindly advice and wisdom to anyone who needs it. A talented painter of landscapes, she's been widowed herself for sixteen years since husband Bill died. Played by accomplished stage and screen actress Anne Haddy, star of the 1970s film *A Town Like Alice* and a host of television shows and series.

OTHER NEIGHBOURS

DES CLARKE The likeable local bank manager, nice guy Des was a total failure with women until he fell head over heels with stripper Daphne Lawrence at a birthday party. Hamfistedly chatting to her afterwards, he discovers she is looking for a new flat and because he needs help to pay the mortgage he invites her to move in – strictly platonically, Des isn't the kind to do anything underhand! But then he set out to court her – and even then he had to fight for her attentions with Shane Ramsay. Eventually he married Daphne and became the proud father of Jamie, before having to cope with Daphne's tragic death. Played by Paul Keane.

EILEEN CLARKE Des's meddling and overpowering mother who somehow believed that the failure of her marriage to husband Malcolm qualified her to interfere in all her son's relationships. Along with Nell Mangel, Eileen is one of Ramsay Street's gossips. She was played by the late Myra de Groot, star of the sixties American comedy 'Bewitched'.

MIKE YOUNG Scott's mate since their schooldays together. Studying teaching at university, Mike also works at the coffee shop in his spare time. He was a victim of terrible child abuse that still haunts him. He was abandoned by his mother Barbara (Diana Greentree) who moved overseas when his father David (Stewart Faichney) died. He then moved in with the Clarkes and has an on/off relationship with Jane Harris. Played by Guy Pearce.

SALLY WELLS She is Des's half-sister – but they were totally unaware that the other existed until she turned up in Erinsborough to search for the father she never knew – who also turns out to be Des's long-lost dad. He invites her to stay, and she takes over the running of the coffee shop. A strikingly pretty girl, she immediately becomes a romantic target of Henry Ramsay, and others. Played by Rowena Mohr.

MALCOLM CLARKE A recent introduction to the cast as Des and Sally's long-lost father. Even though he'd only been living around the corner from Des since he walked out twenty years previously! Re-entered Eileen's life with the intention of remarrying her. Played by Noel Trevarthan, star of stage and television since the 1960s.

DAPHNE LAWRENCE Smart, strong and fiercely independent girl from a rich but uncaring family. She becomes a stripper rather than have to ask her mother Tina for a handout. Runs the coffee shop at Lassiters and eventually marries Des Clarke and bears him his  child. She is reunited at last with her family when she hears her father Allen is dying and she goes home to nurse him. She was played by Elaine Smith ('playing a stripper means you have to look good!') until her sudden demise this summer.

CLIVE GIBBONS Cheerful and slightly whacky, Clive ran an outrageous message delivery service.

Once a promising doctor, he rediscovered his love for medicine during a serious relationship. So he requalified, and eventually left the series apparently to move to a practice in the outback. He was played by Geoff Paine, a very experienced theatre actor whose hobbies include dancing, cycling, skiing, and walking in the Bush. He quit the show after it became a major BBC hit to move to London with his girlfriend and to try to find success on British stage and television. The couple lived in London's Earls Court area, known as the capital's unofficial 'Little Sydney' because so many Australians live there. But it didn't work out and they've now returned Down Under.

NELL MANGEL Never addressed by her christian name because she is so frosty and disliked by the residents of Ramsay Street, this gossiping, interfering old busybody is referred to by everyone as 'Mrs Mangel'. She is doubly disliked by the local youngsters because she is forever telling tales and spying on them while all the time insisting she is 'a good Christian' and that she is doing it for the best of motives. Mrs Mangel was shattered and astonished when her husband Len ran off with his mistress. But no one who knew them was surprised – she made the poor man's life hell with her constant moaning and whingeing. Not even her own daughter Amanda (played by actress Briony Behets) or son-in-law Peter like her very much. Mrs Mangel works as housekeeper at Lassiters Hotel, and is in a state of constant warfare with Madge Ramsay. She defies everyone's attempts to be nice to her, even when she is terrorised by burglars. She was played with great style by the very different Vivean Gray until, as we shall discover later, she quit. English-born Vivean is a spinster who didn't take up acting until her mid-twenties shortly before she emigrated to Australia. She played a similar role to Mrs Mangel in an early Aussie soap opera 'The Sullivans'.

JANE HARRIS Mrs Mangel's granddaughter, she came to live in Erinsborough when her parents moved overseas. When she first went to the local school she was nicknamed 'Plain Jane Super Brain' because she was very mousey and a bit of a bookworm. She was dowdy, lonely and quiet – until Charlene decided to take her under her wing. Ramsay Street was astonished by the beautiful butterfly that emerged from this previously colourless chrysalis, for she was truly lovely and immediately began breaking all the guys' hearts! Mrs Mangel, of course, did not approve of this sudden change and Jane got a lot of criticism from her pompous grandparent when she became a model for a while, and even more when she started dating Mike Young and most of the other good-looking men around the street. Now she works as receptionist for the Daniels Corporation at the hotel. Mrs Mangel doesn't approve of that either!

Jane is played by real-life former model and genuine beauty Annie Jones (who is Hungarian born and now regrets dropping her real name Annika Jasko). She previously appeared in 'Sons and Daughters', a movie called *Run Chrissie Run*, and a number of pop videos.

ROB LEWIS A nice ordinary guy with very simple tastes, though a bit too fond of both his favourite beer – Tooheys – and betting. He is a Waterhole regular. He is a mechanical genius, however, and having worked on the professional motor-racing circuit around the world can quickly strip, repair and rebuild virtually any car. He arrived to manage the garage after his (unseen) wife Brenda died. Shortly after he arrived he set his cap at Madge but to no avail. Played by Ernie Bourne.

GAIL LEWIS She arrived in Erinsborough with her father Rob, but already knew Paul Robinson because they once worked together as airline flight attendants. Both had developed into talented ambitious high-flyers in business. Initially it was not a warm reunion, but eventually as they worked alongside each other for the Daniels Corporation they realised there was something special between them and eventually they married. However, sparks fly continually both in their working and their home lives. Gail is a much nicer person than her husband, and she gets genuinely upset by his attempts to become Ramsay Street's version of notorious JR Ewing. Gail is played by lovely dark-haired Fiona Corke, who despite her youth is in fact a very experienced actress who has appeared in a number of famous Australian TV series. One thing both women have in common is intelligence – Fiona is a university graduate.

HAROLD BISHOP It's been a tough life for poor Harold, and it's left him nervous, shy and a worrier.

He doesn't drink, doesn't smoke, doesn't eat meat and 'conservative' could be his middle name. His first wife Mavis died tragically while they lived in Queensland, leaving him to bring up their two children. But he sees ungrateful son David (played by Kevin Harrington) only rarely and daughter Susan not at all. Then he lost all his money in a stock market crash. He came back to his hometown to try and rebuild his life, and met up again with his childhood sweetheart Madge Ramsay. Something sparked once more and they began dating again. What will become of the relationship? You will find out in a later chapter.

Harold is played by highly experienced actor Ian Smith. He is a multi-talented man – he can play the violin, he is a flyfisherman, was co-producer of a famous Australian drama series, and is a well-known TV scriptwriter too. (He does write for 'Neighbours' but never for scenes involving Harold.)

BEVERLY MARSHALL A relative newcomer to Ramsay Street, she turned up from Adelaide as the GP who replaced Clive Gibbons when he went walkabout from the doctor's surgery. Now she is having an intense and frequently difficult relationship with Jim Robinson as well as running her busy practice. Among her major cases in the coming year will be Jim's lovely mum-in-law Helen Daniels. Beverly finds her when she's suffered a stroke and saves her life, earning Jim's undying gratitude. Even so their relationship runs into troubled waters.

No such difficulties in the life of Lisa

Armytage, who plays Beverly. She is happily married to a lawyer, with two children Rosita and Danika. British-born, she started her acting career with BBC Radio and the theatre in London before moving to Australia and developing an acting career in television.

TODD LANDERS Played by Kristian Schmid, Beverly's cheekily independent nephew followed his aunt from Adelaide to the Ramsay Street neighbourhood to get away from his bullying father, an out-of-work ex-Vietnam War veteran who reckons the world owes him a living and his children should finance his drinking habits.

KATIE LANDERS Todd's sister Katie, who tagged along with him to Erinsborough. She is very insecure, and has a tendency to be a troublemaker. Played by Sally Jensen.

7

DO YOU REALLY KNOW YOUR NEIGHBOURS?

Eighteen million people in Britain suffer from 'Neighbours' Mania. Five days a week they take a walk down Ramsay Street, then spend Saturday and Sunday chewing their nails waiting impatiently for their next instalment on Monday. If asked, most Erinsborough addicts would tell you happily that they know everything there is to know about the Neighbours and what has happened to them since the show was first screened in Britain in October 1986. But do they really? Are *you* a 'Neighbours' expert? We are going to test your 'Neighbours' knowledge to the limit by recalling some of the drama and comedy that has happened down Ramsay Street during some recent and some not to recent episodes. Then we are going to pose some pertinent questions which will reveal once and for all whether or not you can truly claim to be a 'Neighbours' Know-all! The answers are at the end of the chapter.

1 It is shy bank manager Des Clarke's stag night. And his Ramsay Street pals, determined to give him a huge send-off on his way to the altar, hire a sexy stripper. She causes a sensation, and by 2am there is a loud raucous party still going strong at Number 28 Ramsay Street. Two doors away Max

Ramsay gets fed up with the racket and marches round to break up the party, send the stripper packing, and put Des to bed with a bottle of whisky for company. He wakes up the next morning to a pounding head – and to hear pounding on his front door. He opens it to find his bride-to-be Lorraine Kingham standing there with her parents. What does she tell him?

2 Clive Gibbons was the court jester of Ramsay Street, the model on which the character of Charlene's zany brother Henry was later based. It was he who invented a pancake competition to raise money – and customers – for Daphne's café when it hit a rough patch. A former doctor, he gave up practising medicine because of the pressure to start up a whole series of whacky and way-out businesses. Not least was his animal-gram agency, which outraged many of his older Neighbours – he regularly roamed the neighbourhood dressed as a gorilla. But the final straw for Max Ramsay was when he started giving Sunday morning lessons to his staff on how to act as chicken-grams! What did Max do about it?

3 The way Kylie Minogue got her nickname 'bruiser' among the 'Neighbours' cast is well-documented. There was a scene when her character Charlene had a row with Scott (Jason Donovan) in the early days of their romance and she blew her top and punched him. Obviously, Kylie was meant to 'fake' the blow but she misjudged completely. And in fact she not only connected with a haymaking right cross but actually knocked offguard Jason flat, hurting him a lot and cutting his lip! But that famous incident wasn't the first time Charlene punched a fella in 'Neighbours'.

In fact, she really arrived with a bang, for it happened in her very first 'Neighbours' scene. (Kylie was only supposed to be in 'Neighbours' for twelve weeks at first, but proved to be such a knockout she soon became the star of the show.) Her victim was walking home late at night when he spotted a shadowy figure that was in fact Charlene on the Ramsays' balcony. Because it was dark and her hair was up under a hat he couldn't tell whether it was male or female. But because she seemed to be climbing out of a window he thought it was a burglar.

He bravely raced up the stairs to tackle the thief. Charlene thought it was a mugger, punched and screamed at him, her hat fell off and the bruised guy realised it was a girl. Only then did he discover that the 'burglar' was the daughter of a neighbour visiting Ramsay Street for the first time who had mistakenly gone to the wrong house. Who was he?

4 Paul Robinson's first marriage to Terri Inglis ended in heartache, attempted murder and inevitable divorce – but in fact it even began in disaster. For Terri didn't really love Paul anyway. She was actually still pining for her former boyfriend Shane who just happened to be Paul's best man and going out with her supposed best friend Daphne Lawrence. Terri spent most of the ceremony and wedding reception cow-eyed over him. Paul in the

DO YOU KNOW YOUR NEIGHBOURS?

meantime had his own problems getting to the alter. Then an air steward with Qantas, he was stranded in Singapore due to a technical hitch and looked set to miss the ceremony altogether. Unluckily for him – for Terri was later to trick him out of his money and attempt to have him killed! – he made it. But at the wedding reception things got even worse. Shane got drunk and flew into a rage and started boasting about how badly he treated Daphne. What happened next?

5 Every kid dreams of being discovered by a talent scout and becoming a famous pop star. Well, Scott Robinson and his best pal Mike Young thought their daydreams had come true when they fell for a cruel practical joke by bitchy Sue Parker. She never forgave Mike for preferring Jane Harris to her, and vowed to get even. She heard around the school they all attended that Scott and Mike had written a pop song and had sent it off to rock star Monk McCallum.

So Sue posed as McCallum's secretary to invite them to go and see him and sing the number to him personally. They not only fell for it, but they then even made a special demo tape of themselves singing the song and co-opted Charlene into adding the back-up vocals. They couldn't resist telling their schoolpals about their big break, and the news spread like wildfire. But when they turned up for their supposed appointment at McCallum's house they discovered it was a cruel hoax. They left the tape anyway, but then slunk home with their tails between their legs – only to meet gloating Sue Parker who publicly rubbed it in that they had made fools of themselves. But what was the surprise outcome of it all?

6 Jane Harris, nickednamed 'Plain Jane Super Brain' when she joined the regulars of Ramsay Street, was a shy, retiring girl who was intimidated and browbeaten by everyone from her grandmother Mrs Mangel to her classmates at school. She wore granny-style spectacles, make-up was unknown to her, and from her clothes you could barely tell what sex she was never mind whether she had a figure. But then Charlene took a shine to her, and decided to change her image completely. First she lent her some of her own clothes, taught her how to use make-up and even totally changed her hairstyle. The transformation was stunning – and Mike Young fell for her immediately. Later so did Henry Ramsay. She became a confident, poised young woman, and it was all thanks to Charlene. How did Jane repay her kindness?

7 Madge Mitchell hates the fact that her son Henry has got a criminal record – so she is horrified when she in turn is accused of theft by Paul Robinson and it is all Henry's fault! The trouble starts when Henry is drinking with a criminal acquaintance in The Waterhole. He pays for a round with a $50 bill.

Then the crook buys a drink and insists he paid with a $50 bill as well. A till check reveals just one such banknote, which the villain 'proves' is his by reciting the last three digits. But Madge has admitted taking a $50 note from her son. So why is there just one? Manager Paul Robinson accuses Madge of theft and threatens to call the police. So how does ex-jailbird Henry turn detective and save the day – and his mum's reputation?

Marriage and Des Clarke didn't go together. Four times he had been due to marry, four times he had been let down on his wedding day. So he kept even his toes crossed when he finally got to the altar with Daphne Lawrence. Throughout the ceremony, throughout the reception he waited in terror for the disaster he was convinced would strike. How could he really expect to find happiness at last? But it all went wonderfully. Even Clive Gibbons didn't turn up to read the telegrams wearing a gorilla outfit as he had feared. And then it was off on a wonderful honeymoon with the beautiful young bride he still couldn't quite believe had agreed to become his wife. They had two wonderful loving days at their honeymoon hotel, filled with an almost primitive passion for each other. And then what disaster struck?

9 It is tough when you've only got one parent and then someone else comes into their life and starts to take some of the attention that you are used to getting. That's what happened to little Lucy Robinson when her handsome widowed father Jim met Zoe Davis. She was his businessman son Paul's secretary and despite a twenty-year age difference they soon began dating. And Lucy, aged just twelve, was jealous. Her resentment was fuelled by big brother Paul's obvious similar distaste. Though that was due in part at least to the fact that he had tried and failed to date Zoe!

So Lucy set out to do everything she could to wreck the romance, from being downright offensive to dumping a jug of water on Zoe's lap in the middle of dinner. And after her daddy took Zoe away for a weekend her bitterness went into overdrive. Zoe began receiving mystery phonecalls at work. When she answered them no one would speak, or she would just hear heavy breathing. It was Lucy, of course – and it began to work. Zoe got rattled and frightened, disrupting her job and causing rows with Jim because she was so strung up about it. But then Zoe got a policeman's whistle – and the next mystery call she received she blew it full blast down the telephone at the mystery caller. What was the result?

10 Scott Robinson and Jane Harris are both very attractive young people – so it's not surprising that they are invited by Lassiters to become models for a line of equipment they plan to market. They need some photographs for advertising both in local newspapers and for posters to put up in the area. It causes some aggro both with Charlene and with Jane's boyfriend Mike Young because they are nervous of their respective partners being thrown together in such intimate circumstances. And of course Scott can't resist making a big deal out of the offer and winding feisty Charlene up about it all.

One of the modelling assignments is to pose with watergear, and the photographer decides not unnaturally that perhaps the pictures should be taken on the local lake. He assures them it will be perfectly safe. But when they turn up on the day it turns out to be blowing a gale and the promised 'motorlaunch' turns out to be little more than a rowing boat with an outboard motor on the back. Suddenly the glitter of modelling starts to look distinctly tarnished. What happens when they get out into the middle of the water?

ANSWERS

1) She arrived to tell him the wedding was off. Later stripper Daphne turned up to reclaim a mislaid earring, which started a long chain of events that ended with *her* marrying Des.

2) Max Ramsay played a deafening tape-recording of animal noises outside Clive's bedroom window in the

early hours of the morning. But Clive was away – and Max upset the rest of Ramsay Street instead.

3) It was Scott! After the fuss calmed down he took her in, gave her a cuppa, guided her to the right house, and asked for a date!

4) Shane started a terrible brawl when Daphne's old pal Mark Keating (played by Stephen Lawson) objected to the way he ill-treated her. And Shane came off worst – he ended up face down in a cake, lost the fight, and at last long-suffering Daphne left him in disgust.

5) Shades of real-life! McCallum's manager turns up to say the song is promising and that the boys should keep writing, but that the real talent is Charlene's back-up vocals. He advises a pop career for her!

6) Jane becomes the Vamp of Ramsay Street, makes a play for recently married Scott, and is found by Charlene in a passionate clinch with her husband.

7) Henry discovers his 'pal' had memorised the last three digits of *his* $50 note. He finds the guy's sister who comes forward to tell Paul it is an old scam of her brother's.

8) Des plays Tarzan, sweeps Daphne off her feet to carry her off to bed, slips a disc and spends the rest of the honeymoon in agony!

9) The whistle bursts Lucy's eardrum and she ends up in hospital. But Zoe realises she can't win her over and refuses to wed Jim.

10) The boat capsizes and it is feared Scott has drowned. But he actually swims ashore without being seen.

QUICKIE QUIZ

1) What forced Shane to give up his bid to become an Olympic diving champ?

2) Which other TV show did Kylie Minogue and Jason Donovan appear in together before 'Neighbours'?

3) What is Jamie Clarke's middle name?

4) Most people with long names get them shortened by their pals. What do the Ramsay Street gang call Charlene?

5) Do you know what Helen Daniels' chauffeur service is called?

6) Which song did Charlene and Scott have playing at their wedding?

7) Who is Jim Robinson's partner in their engineering firm?

8) Which local paper for Ramsay Street residents does Scott start his journalism apprenticeship with?

9) Who did Mike Young dump for Jane Harris?

10) When Charlene walked out on her mum, what did she live in at Lassiters?

11) What school subject did Jane Harris coach Scott in?

12) How is Charlene Mitchell related to Shane Ramsay?

13) Who was Scott's boss in the coffee shop?

14) What was the name of the parrot that Daphne gave to Lucy Robinson?

15) Who broke up Paul Robinson and Susan Meadows?

16) Before they even decided to get married, what did Scott and Charlene do that shocked the neighbourhood?

17) How did Paul Robinson meet first wife Terri Inglis?

18) What is Mrs Mangel's 'psychic' talent?

19) Who saved Charlene when the caravan blew up?

20) Who tried to come between Madge Mitchell and Harold Bishop?

QUICKIE QUIZ ANSWERS

1) Injuries suffered in a car crash.

2) They were brother and sister in the Australian TV show 'The Crawfords'.

3) His full name is Jamie Kingsley Clarke.

4) Charlene is chopped to Lenny.

5) It is the 'Home James' chauffeur service.

6) The song was 'Suddenly' by the Australian pop group Rose Tattoo.

7) Ross Warner.

8) The local paper is the *Erinsborough News*.

9) Nikki Dennison is the loser in love.

10) She lived there in a caravan.

11) Jane coached Scott in maths.

12) Shane is Charlene's cousin.

13) Wally.

14) The parrot is called Squawker.

15) Clive Gibbons stole Susan Meadows.

16) They lived together in a trial marriage to discover if it would work out if they wed for real.

17) She was plumber Max Ramsay's apprentice.

18) Mrs Mangel reckons she can read tea-leaves.

19) Good old Scott, of course – even though they were quarrelling at the time. He discovered someone had rigged up a bomb as a prank to blow the caravan up while Charlene was at school, but she had played truant and gone back early. He raced round there to save her in the nick of time.

20) It was Gail's father, Rob Lewis.

8

NEIGHBOURS – THE FUTURE

Will television's Marriage of the Year in 1988 survive 1989? Can Madge find happiness at last with Harold? How will Des survive now that Daphne is dead? And is there life after 'Neighbours' for the stars who have decided to quit the world's most successful soap opera?

Very briefly, the answers are: no; partly; with difficulty; and sometimes. But if you want to know more detail of what has happened and what is going to happen to your Ramsay Street favourite then read on ...

KYLIE MINOGUE Is there anyone who doesn't know that the girl who plays apprentice motor-mechanic Charlene became one of the world's most successful and highly paid pop stars in 1988, at one stage pocketing an estimated $1.3m (£620,000) in a single month from record royalties?

But the question is, will she return to 'Neighbours' where she first made her name? The answer is yes for a few weeks, then she will disappear for good. The only possibility of her returning is if her pop career nose-dives – which is of course a possibility in that notoriously fickle industry.

But her departure could hardly be more dramatic. Her marriage to Scott gets into difficulty over his immaturity. Then a stranger called Steve Fisher appears on the scene, and she finds herself falling madly in lust with him. She knows that deep down she loves Scott, but she finds it almost impossible to control her physical hunger for the stranger – who knows exactly what effect he is having on Charlene and tries to take advantage by pursuing her relentlessly. Scott realises something is going on – and turns for consolation to Charlene's former best friend turned vamp Jane Harris ...

Meanwhile, in real life, as well as continuing to make records, Kylie is to play her first part in a TV mini-series called 'The Silence of Dean Maitland' in which she plays a teenage girl who has an affair with a catholic priest. But Kylie vows, 'There are no raunchy scenes, I wouldn't do anything like that.'

JASON DONOVAN He will be on British screens for a long time yet, as Scott tries to save his marriage, has that affair with Jane Harris, and tries to build his career as a journalist with the local paper. But Jason was spending more and more time away from Ramsay Street. He finally quit – though the door has been left open for him to return some day. This is because he is also pursuing a music career like real-life girlfriend Kylie Minogue and is frequently touring the world to promote his records. He will in fact spend much of the summer in Britain trying to make his lucrative music career really take off and plans to buy a house in London. In the meantime he took off three months at the end of last year to record a major role in a TV wartime mini-series called 'Heroes'. And he is hopeful that the drama's success will open the door to more such serious work. However, the possibility is that he will re-sign for another 'Neighbours' season. And he will be on British TV screens for at least another year.

STEFAN DENNIS His character Paul Robinson may be a whizz at business but he is a real loser in love. His first marriage failed when his wife tried to murder him, and now second wife Gail – played by Fiona Corke – is threatening to walk out for good. The marital problems start in earnest when they join a test-tube baby scheme in a desperate bid to have a child.

In real life, Stefan is having a second crack at a pop career after his first record 'Don't It Make You Feel Good' flopped. Fiona Corke is considering quitting 'Neighbours' to go back into more serious acting.

ANNIE JONES Brought in to replace Kylie Minogue as the main love interest in the show, her character Jane Harris proves to be much raunchier and man-hungry than Charlene ever was! After enticing Scott, dallying with teacher Mike Young before dumping him and giving Henry the come-on, she meets a wealthy American called Mark Grainger. He wants to marry her, and she even makes her wedding dress and all the arrangements. But at the last minute she can't go through with it – and sets her cap at another Ramsay Street regular.

PAUL KEANE His character Des has had more than his fair share of bad luck. First, wife Daphne became severely ill with post-natal depression after their baby Jamie was born, putting him through torture, then she got killed in a horrific car smash. Des becomes so desperately lonely and despairing that he turns to drink.

Eventually he really hits rock bottom and even considers suicide. But he doesn't go through with it for the baby's sake. Instead he hires Bronwyn (Rachel Friend) as his nanny and joins a computer dating agency in a bid to find himself a new wife and son Jamie a new mum. He has a string of disastrous dates or brief encounters, none of which prove suitable. Then nice guy Des begins to fall under the spell of Ramsay Street's resident man-eater Jane Harris and it seems certain even more heartache is on the way ...

ANNE CHARLESTON Madge and Harold get hitched at last! The tragic death of Daphne makes them look afresh at their long romance and so they decide the time is right for a full-blown wedding. Henry gives his mum away, Jim Robinson is best man, and Jane Harris a bridesmaid along with Charlene. The 'Neighbours' wedding comes complete with four-piece band, five-tiered wedding cake and full slap-up wedding reception.

But marriage has a rough ride down Ramsay Street – witness the way Scott and Charlene hit the rocks. And amazingly these two former childhood sweethearts begin to have marriage problems of their own.

In real life, Anne Charleston is having problems of her own too with the taxman. For she claims that Australia's Inland Revenue department is picking on the stars of the cast – including Kylie Minogue – and going through their financial affairs with a fine toothcomb simply because they are so famous.

CRAIG McLACHLAN The man who has really caught the public's imagination as Henry Ramsay continues to lurch from daft scheme to crazy crisis. He has an off/on relationship with Bronwyn (played by lovely Rachel Friend) which proves to be a real knockout  the night he turns up for a candlelit dinner for two half drunk and switches on the TV. A row starts, he storms out into the garden and into a tree, which knocks him out cold. He comes to to find her sobbing gently, 'I love you'.

He then takes her in his arms and it looks as if her dreams have at last come true. But a week later he turns up with another girlfriend and breaks her heart once more.

In real life Craig too is hunting stardom in the pop scene. He and two pals will spend summer 1989 in Britain playing gigs around the clubs and music pubs of London in a bid to find a record deal. He and wife Karen suddenly split just before Christmas 1988 and he is romancing ... Rachel Friend!

ALAN DALE It's a busy year for the man who plays Jim Robinson, both on and off-screen. For in real life he got engaged recently to his girlfriend, former Miss

Australia Tracey Pearson – at twenty-three, she is virtually half his age – and they plan to marry this year. He will pay for it from his $3000 a week salary, for he is the highest paid 'Neighbours' star.

He has also got married on-screen, to doctor wife Beverly. But things run anything but smoothly and she leaves him to go back to her parents in Perth and rethink their relationship.

93

GUY PEARCE Let's hope he has more luck in his private life than Mike Young does down Ramsay Street. In months to come he knuckles down and becomes a teacher – only to risk losing everything he has worked for when pupil Bronwyn (Rachel Friend) decides to seduce him! She sweet-talks him into giving her private tuition and helping her with her homework, then successfully turns · on the charm. But after just a few secret dates, they're spotted by nosey parker Mrs Mangel who promptly informs the girl's father! Bronwyn is sent to live with relatives for several weeks and Mike has to fight hard to persuade the school headmaster not to fire him.

PETER O'BRIEN and ELAINE SMITH. After Kylie Minogue and Jason Donovan, undoubtedly the best-known deserters from 'Neighbours'. Peter left to become a star of the rival Australian TV serial 'Flying Doctors' (shown on prime-time Saturday night television in Britain). Then he flew to Britain to star in a Christmas pantomine at Stockport in Cheshire with his girlfriend Elaine. But in real life Elaine quit 'Neighbours' a year ago and is now happy to slipstream along with boyfriend Peter while he decides whether to base his career in Britain or whether to return to Australia.

They lived in Stockport during their panto run, but since it ended have rented a house just near the River Thames in exclusive Putney. While Peter tours Britain with another stage play or goes back to Australia to film 'Flying Doctors', she is happy to stay at home, take the occasional stage role and take their dog for a walk along the riverside or on Putney Heath.

VIVEAN GRAY The character Mrs Mangel has become one of the most disliked in any soap opera – and eventually the unpleasant public identification of her in real life with the part she plays became just too much for Vivean to take and she quit.

But at least the scriptwriters allow her to leave in a nice way; Nell Mangel meets an old school boyfriend who falls in love with her and whisks her away to a new life on the other side of Australia! It is another beautiful 'Neighbours' wedding with all the trimmings and with her niece Jane Harris the chief bridesmaid.

In real life a gentle and cultured lady, she now lives quietly in a beautiful house outside Melbourne with her three pedigree cats trying to improve her piano-playing and devoting much time to her hobby of photography. She also plans to travel, mainly to the Middle East which she has adored ever since a magnificent holiday cruise down the Nile.

She says, 'I loved "Neighbours", and the rest of the cast were marvellous. But because it was so successful I could barely set foot outside my door without someone screaming abuse at horrid old "Mrs Mangel". People didn't seem to appreciate that it was only acting. So I decided to take a break. But the scriptwriters have very kindly left the door open for me to return if I wish. So who knows? Perhaps one day Mrs Mangel will be back down Ramsay Street ...'